American Indian
Art and Culture

CHEROKEE

Heather Kissock
and Rachel Small

WEIGL PUBLISHERS INC.
"Creating Inspired Learning"
www.weigl.com

Published by Weigl Publishers Inc.
350 5th Avenue, 59th Floor
New York, NY 10118

Website: www.weigl.com

Library of Congress Cataloging-in-Publication Data

Kissock, Heather.
 Cherokee : American Indian art and culture / Heather Kissock and Rachel Small.
    p. cm.
 Includes index.
 ISBN 978-1-60596-994-7 (hardcover : alk. paper) -- ISBN 978-1-60596-995-4 (softcover : alk. paper) -- ISBN 978-1-60596-996-1 (e-book)
 1. Cherokee art--Juvenile literature. 2. Cherokee Indians--Material culture--Juvenile literature. 3. Cherokee Indians--Social life and customs--Juvenile literature. I. Small, Rachel. II. Title.
 E99.C5K53 2011
 970.004'97--dc22
                          2010005335

Printed in the United States of America in North Mankato, Minnesota
1 2 3 4 5 6 7 8 9 0 14 13 12 11 10

042010
WEP264000

Photograph and Text Credits
Cover: Courtesy, National Museum of the American Indian, Smithsonian Institution (18/9357); Alamy: pages 4, 7, 8, 12, 13, 14, 16T, 21; Courtesy of the Bata Shoe Museum: page 9B; Corbis: pages 5, 6, 17, 20; Dreamstime: page 11L; Getty Images: pages 10, 11M, 11R, 15, 23; Courtesy of the National Museum of the American Indian, Smithsonian Institution: page 16B; Nativestock: pages 9T, 9M;

 **PROJECT COORDINATOR** Heather Kissock

DESIGN Terry Paulhus

 **ILLUSTRATOR** Martha Jablonski-Jones

Contents

The People

The Cherokee Indians are from the southeast part of the United States. Their **traditional** lands covered what are now the states of Tennessee and Kentucky, as well as parts of Georgia, North Carolina, South Carolina, and Virginia.

As Europeans settled these areas, the Cherokee began moving west. They arrived in Texas in the early 1800s and settled in the southeast part of the state. Here, the land was good for growing crops. More Europeans moved to the area, and by the mid-1800s, the Cherokee were forced to move to what is now the state of Oklahoma. Today, there are more than 300,000 Cherokee in the United States. Many still live in Oklahoma.

NET LINK

Find out why the Cherokee were forced to leave Texas at **www.texasindians.com/cherokee.htm**.

Cherokee Homes

MUD HOMES

Long ago, the Cherokee lived in small houses made from wood, bark, mud, and clay. Most Cherokee lived in villages that had 30 to 60 homes.

Cherokee Ideas

Cherokee villages often had palisades around them. These high fences protected the Cherokee from attack.

LOG CABINS

Later, they lived in windowless log cabins. Many generations of families lived together.

Cherokee Clothing

SKIRTS AND PONCHOS

Cherokee women traditionally wore wraparound skirts with **poncho**-like tops. These were made from deerskin or woven **fibers**. After Europeans arrived in the area, the women began wearing skirts, blouses, and dresses made from cotton.

BREECHCLOTHS AND LEGGINGS

Long ago, Cherokee men wore **breechcloths** and leggings. These clothes were usually made from deerskin. After Europeans arrived, the Cherokee began wearing beaded jackets as well.

CAPES AND CLOAKS

The Cherokee wore capes during important ceremonies. These capes were traditionally made of turkey feathers. Cloaks made from animal hides kept the Cherokee warm in winter.

JEWELRY

Some Cherokee made jewelry from sterling silver, leather, beads, and shells.

MOCCASINS

Leather moccasins kept the heat in during the winter and protected the Cherokees' feet.

Hunting and Gathering

SQUASH

Squash was just one of the many vegetables the Cherokee grew in their gardens. It was often used to make soups and breads.

CORN

Corn was used in many foods. Sometimes, it was eaten fresh. It could also be dried to make flour for bread and other dishes.

BEANS

Beans were another vegetable the Cherokee grew. They, too, were used to make breads and could be put in soups and stews.

The Cherokee were mainly farmers. They grew crops for much of their food. For meat and fish, however, the men would hunt the lands and fish the local waters. Women would pick berries and nuts when in season.

BEARS

Bears could be found throughout Cherokee lands. The meat was cooked and eaten on its own or put in stews.

ELK

Elk was an important part of the Cherokee diet. Like bear meat, elk was cooked on its own or added to stews.

NUTS AND BERRIES

Nuts and berries were used to sweeten dishes and give them more flavor.

Cherokee Tools

SCRAPERS

The Cherokee used a variety of tools. Some, such as scrapers, were used to prepare hides for **tanning**. Scrapers could be made out of stone, wood, or bone. Axes were used to chop wood. The blade of the ax was usually made from granite. The handle was made of wood.

HUNTING

The bow and arrow was an important tool for the Cherokee. It was used to hunt large animals, such as deer. **Flint** was a good material for making arrows. It is very hard, but easy to chip. The Cherokee also used **blowguns** to hunt smaller animals, such as raccoons and turkeys.

NET LINK

See how a Cherokee blowgun works by visiting **http://video.google.com/ videoplay?docid=-904664033367384180#**.

Moving from Place to Place

HORSES

Traditionally, the Cherokee traveled the land by foot. When Europeans brought horses, the Cherokee began riding them from place to place. Horses were also used to pull wagons.

To hollow a log, the Cherokee covered it with clay and set it on fire. When the clay burned off, they cut out the burned wood. This was a long process. It could take several months to complete one canoe.

CANOES

The Cherokee traditionally used dugout canoes to travel on water. These canoes were made by removing the insides of a log.

Cherokee Music and Dance

Music played an important role in Cherokee life. Drums and rattles were used for most music. Some Cherokee also played flutes and trumpets. Trumpets were made from animal horns or large shells. Flutes were made from cane.

The Cherokee had many traditional songs that they performed through singing, dancing, or both.

NET LINK

Learn how to do the Cherokee Stomp Dance at **www.youtube.com/watch?v=C5HpNnxEDnE**.

Long ago, when the Cherokee first arrived on Earth, they thought that their lives would be better if there was daylight all the time. They asked the Creator to take away the night, and he did. However, with the Sun shining all the time, their crops burned, and people had problems sleeping.

The people asked the Creator to take away the Sun and let them live with moonlight all the time. The Creator agreed and did what he was asked. Soon, it became very cold, and the crops stopped growing. There was no food for people to eat. Some people died.

Again, the people went to the Creator and asked him to return both night and day to them. The Creator did as he was asked, and the Cherokee became strong once again.

The Creator felt bad that people had suffered because of his actions. He decided to create a tree called the cedar. Inside the tree, he placed the spirits of the people who had died. To this day, the cedar tree is said to protect the Cherokee against evil spirits. Many Cherokee carry a piece of cedar with them at all times.

Cherokee Art

Traditional Cherokee art was beautiful to look at but also had a purpose. Baskets were used to carry food, such as corn and nuts. Clay pots were used for cooking and to store water.

Cherokee Ideas

The Cherokee used different types of clay to produce pots in many colors. Their pots could be red and white or black and white.

Cherokee women made pots using only clay and their hands. They rolled the clay into long ropes and coiled them to make pots. Potters would sometimes use stones and wooden paddles to carve designs into the pots.

Make Cherokee Bean Bread

Ingredients
  1 cup cornmeal
  1/2 cup flour
  2 teaspoons baking powder
  1 tablespoon sugar
  2 cups milk
  1/4 cup melted shortening
  1 beaten egg
  2 tablespoons honey
  4 cups drained brown beans

Instructions
1. Mix all of the ingredients, except the beans.
2. Fold in the beans.
3. Pour into greased pan.
4. Bake at 450° Fahrenheit for 30 minutes.
5. Serve warm, and enjoy.

Glossary

blowguns: pipes through which darts are blown by the breath

breechcloths: cloths that cover the lower part of men's bodies

fibers: long, thin threads

flint: a piece of hard stone

poncho: a cloak that has a hole in the center that a person's head can come through

tanning: turning animal skins into leather

traditional: relating to beliefs, practices, and objects that have been passed down from one generation to the next

Index